Why Is the Sky Blue?

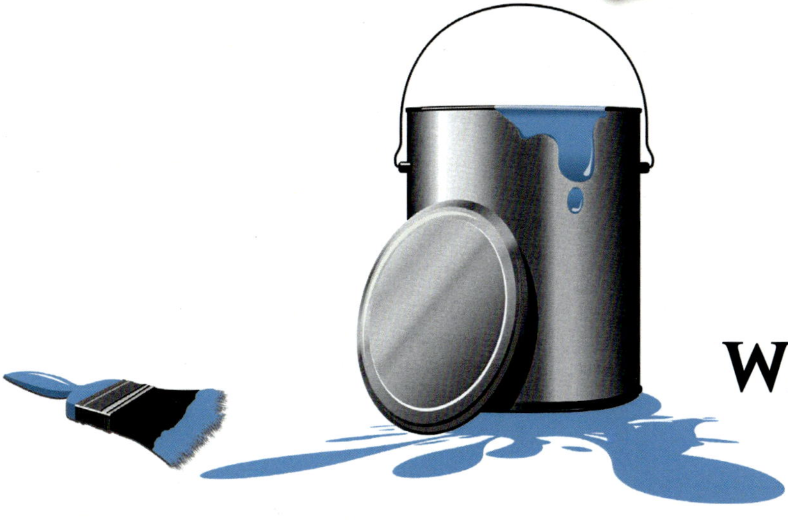

Ruth Owen

WINDMILL BOOKS

Published in 2020 by **Windmill Books**,
an imprint of Rosen Publishing
29 East 21st Street, New York, NY 10010

Copyright © Ruby Tuesday Books Limited 2018

All rights reserved. No part of this book may be reproduced in any form without permission in writing from the publisher, except by a reviewer.

Concept development: Ruby Tuesday Books Ltd

Author: Ruth Owen
Consultant: Josh Barker
Designer: Emma Randall
Editor: Mark J. Sachner
Production: John Lingham

Image Credits:
Images courtesy of Ruby Tuesday Books and Shutterstock.

Ruby Tuesday Books has made every attempt to contact the copyright holder.

Cataloging-in-Publication Data

Names: Owen, Ruth.
Title: Why is the sky blue? / Ruth Owen.
Description: New York : Windmill Books, 2019. | Series: Little scientists, big questions
Identifiers: ISBN 9781725393561 (pbk.) | ISBN 9781725393585 (library bound) | ISBN 9781725393578 (6 pack)
Subjects: LCSH: Sky--Juvenile literature. | Sky--Color--Juvenile literature. | Refraction--Juvenile literature.Classification: LCC QC863.5 O8456 2019 | DDC 520--dc23

Manufactured in the United States of America

CPSIA Compliance Information: Batch #BS19WM:
For Further Information contact Rosen Publishing, New York, New York at 1-800-237-9932

We're going to paint a picture.

To answer our **BIG** question, we need to know about two things that begin with A.

Air Atmosphere

Take a deep **breath**.
You've just breathed in some air.

Get ready for some BIG science!

The air is made up of teeny-tiny floating things called molecules.

Let's say it! "MOLL-uh-kyools"

Most of the molecules are gases with BIG names.

Nitrogen

Oxygen

Argon

Carbon dioxide

Oxygen is a gas that people and animals need to breathe.

There is even air way up here where planes fly.

The thick blanket of air that covers Earth is called the atmosphere.

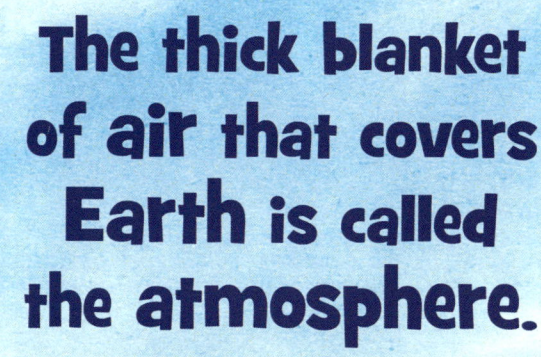

Let's say it! "AT-moss-fear"

The atmosphere goes up . . .

. . . and up and up . . .

. . . for miles into space.

Earth

It's time for some more BIG science!

sunlight

The sun's bright light looks white.

Be safe!

Never look directly at the sun because it will badly damage your eyes. Even sunglasses won't protect your eyes.

But actually the sun's light is made up of different colors.

white light

colors in light

prism

You can see the colors when light shines through a glass shape called a prism.

More BIG science coming up!

The colors that make up sunlight are

- red
- orange
- yellow
- green
- blue
- indigo
- violet

These **colors** are the **colors** of the **rainbow**.

The sun's light shines through Earth's atmosphere.

Remember all those molecules that make the air in the atmosphere?

light

Boing Boing Boing Boing Boing

The light bumps into all the tiny floating molecules.

The light gets bounced and scattered in all directions.

The blue light gets scattered the most.

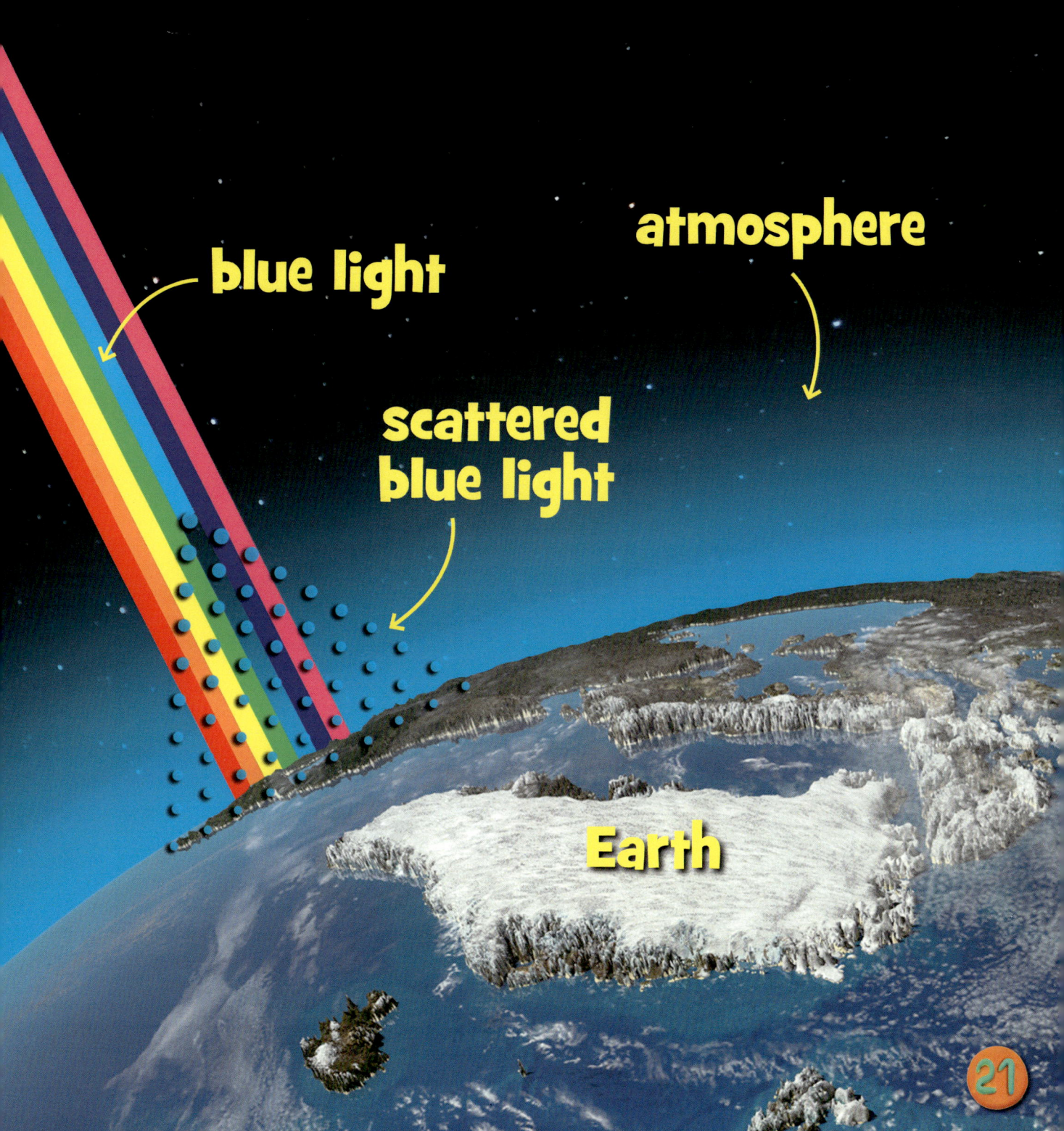

The blue light gets scattered more than all the other colors.

This makes the sky look blue.

Hooray!

My Science Words

air
The gases, such as nitrogen, oxygen, and carbon dioxide, that are all around us on Earth.

atmosphere
A thick blanket of air that surrounds Earth.

molecules
The small parts of substances, such as air and water.

oxygen
An invisible gas that's all around us in the air. People and animals need oxygen to breathe.